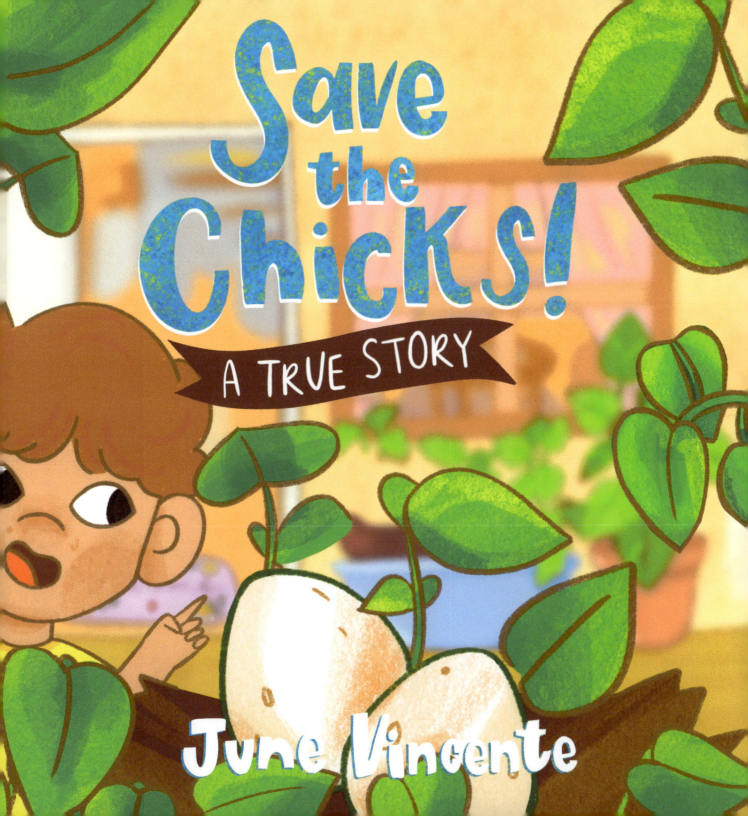

Acknowledgement

It is with appreciation and gratitude that it was Conard Martin who came to be the Project Manager of this creation. He interpreted my vision and breathed life into the written words of my story. His team of illustrators created scene after scene filled with color and colorful characters.
Thank you all:

Joanna Holland, Illustrator
Conard Martin, Project Manager

Hey Mom,
"Look what I found
A bird has left eggs for us
See the nest is on the ground."

The bird flew away,
When I began to fuss.
She will come back today.
I pray.

Chicks will die if temperature's too low.
They need help to survive
Warmth will keep them alive.

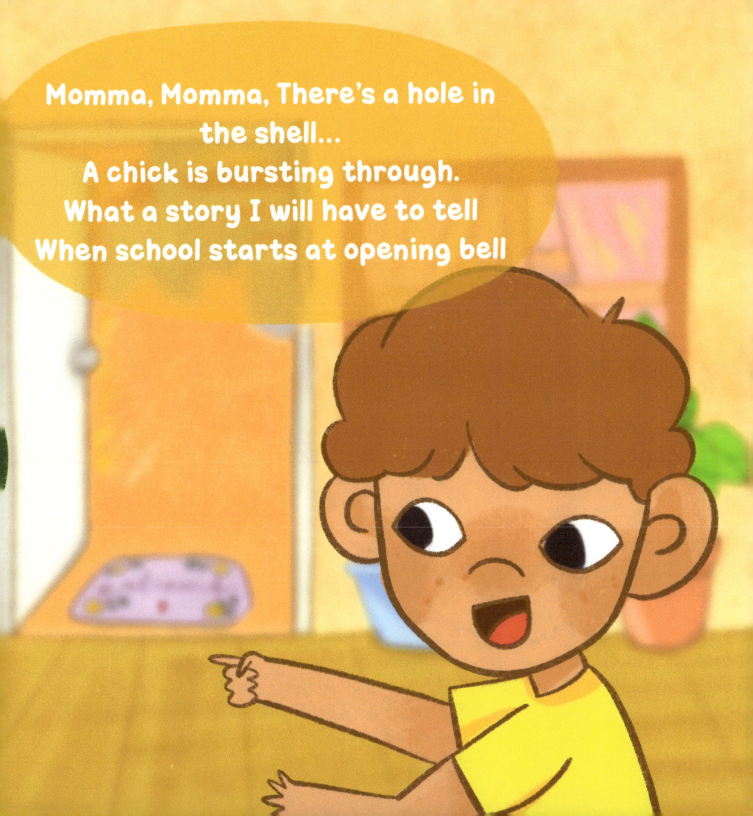

A radio announcement said a storm would arrive bringing rain and freezing cold.

Don't be so bold
When you are told
It would not be a good time to drive.

Noah is brave.
He will save
Little baby chicks.
Momma is worrying
And scurrying
To stop all of Noah's tricks.

There is an old lamp.
I know what I'll do
I'll connect the electric wire,
Plug in the power
And be ready for the cold.
I will bring in the chicks.
Their space will be fixed,
They will be warm in the storm.

"It is time for bed,
So rest your head.
I will be right down the hall."

It fell to the floor with a resounding crash
And the light flickered and died.

No lights, no lamp, no place to hide.
It will be morning before we would see if the chicks survived.
Pray that will be.

Tears falling from crying eyes.
There is only one chick Noah has heard.
Only one chick is a big surprise.

Morning and the sun
Peaks through the trees.
It is warm and quiet
With a gentle breeze.

A chick nestles close to the momma bird.
One chick is all Noah sees

Out of the bushes and behind the mound
The little chick has now been found.

Momma bird with two chicks make three.
Together this happy family.

With their momma bird
Who stayed and waited
For days on the shell
To have this good story
For our children to tell.

The Real Images

Printed in the USA
CPSIA information can be obtained
at www.ICGtesting.com
LVHW061301200124
769429LV00016B/172